Alphabet Books

ABC Under the Sea

An Ocean Life Alphabet Book

by Barbara Knox

Consultant:
Daniel K. Odell, Ph.D.
Senior Research Biologist
Hubbs-SeaWorld Research Institute

Capstone press

Mankato, MN

Aa Bb Cc Dd Ee Ff Gg Hh Ii Jj Kk Ll Mm
Nn Oo Pp Qq Rr Ss Tt Uu Vv Ww Xx Yy Zz

A is for anemone.

Sea anemones are animals that look like plants. They stick to rocks and coral.

Aa **Bb** Cc Dd Ee Ff Gg Hh Ii Jj Kk Ll Mm Nn Oo Pp Qq Rr Ss Tt Uu Vv Ww Xx Yy Zz

B is for brittle star.

Brittle stars can have five to seven arms. If one arm gets cut off, a new arm can grow.

C is for chocolate chip sea star.

Chocolate chip sea stars have spots on their bodies. The spots look like chocolate chips.

4

Aa Bb Cc Dd Ee Ff Gg Hh Ii Jj Kk Ll Mm Nn Oo Pp Qq Rr Ss Tt Uu Vv Ww Xx Yy Zz

Aa Bb Cc **Dd** Ee Ff Gg Hh Ii Jj Kk Ll Mm Nn Oo Pp Qq Rr Ss Tt Uu Vv Ww Xx Yy Zz

D is for dolphin.

Dolphins breathe through blowholes. A dolphin closes its blowhole when it swims underwater.

Aa Bb Cc Dd **Ee** Ff Gg Hh Ii Jj Kk Ll Mm
Nn Oo Pp Qq Rr Ss Tt Uu Vv Ww Xx Yy Zz

E is for eel.

Eels look like snakes. They sometimes hide under rocks during the day.

Aa Bb Cc Dd Ee **Ff** Gg Hh Ii Jj Kk Ll Mm Nn Oo Pp Qq Rr Ss Tt Uu Vv Ww Xx Yy Zz

F is for frogfish.

Frogfish are able to change colors. They can look like other things in the ocean.

Aa Bb Cc Dd Ee Ff Gg Hh Ii Jj Kk Ll Mm
Nn Oo Pp Qq Rr Ss Tt Uu Vv Ww Xx Yy Zz

G is for great white shark.

Great white sharks have very sharp teeth. They bite chunks of food and swallow without chewing.

Aa Bb Cc Dd Ee Ff Gg **Hh** Ii Jj Kk Ll Mm Nn Oo Pp Qq Rr Ss Tt Uu Vv Ww Xx Yy Zz

H is for hermit crab.

Hermit crabs do not have their own shells.
They climb into empty snail shells to live.

Aa Bb Cc Dd Ee Ff Gg Hh **Ii** Jj Kk Ll Mm Nn Oo Pp Qq Rr Ss Tt Uu Vv Ww Xx Yy Zz

I is for indigo hamlet.

Indigo hamlets live near coral reefs. They swim near the bottom. They eat shrimp and other sea creatures.

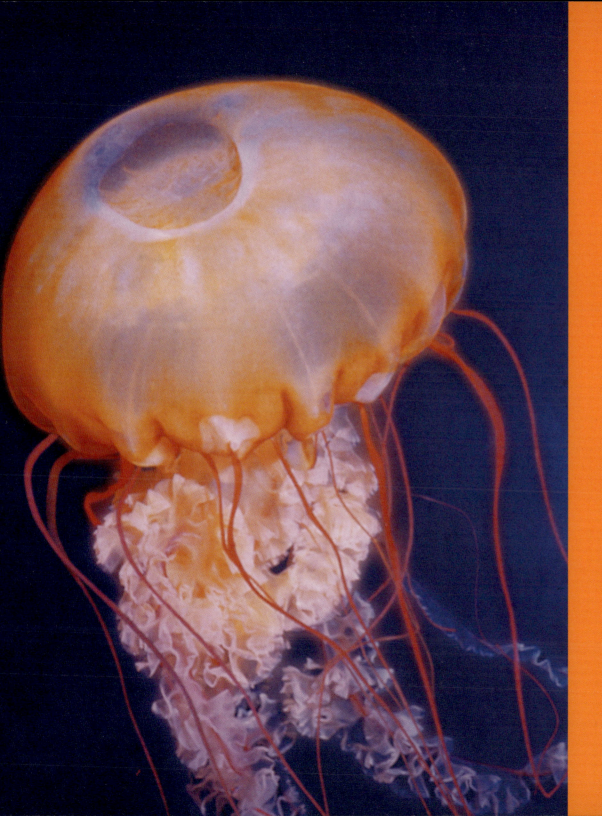

Aa Bb Cc Dd Ee Ff Gg Hh Ii Jj Kk Ll Mm
Nn Oo Pp Qq Rr Ss Tt Uu Vv Ww Xx Yy Zz

J is for jellyfish.

Jellyfish have no eyes, brain, heart, or bones. They move by pumping water in and out of their bodies.

K is for killer whale.

Killer whales are called orcas. The killer whale is the largest member of the dolphin family.

Aa Bb Cc Dd Ee Ff Gg Hh Ii Jj Kk Ll Mm Nn Oo Pp Qq Rr Ss Tt Uu Vv Ww Xx Yy Zz

L is for lionfish.

Lionfish have many spines. The spines sting other fish that come too close.

Aa Bb Cc Dd Ee Ff Gg Hh Ii Jj Kk Ll **Mm**
Nn Oo Pp Qq Rr Ss Tt Uu Vv Ww Xx Yy Zz

M is for manatee.

Manatees are mammals with thick, wrinkled skin. They eat only plants.

N is for needlefish.

Needlefish have long, thin bodies.
They look like sewing needles.

Aa Bb Cc Dd Ee Ff Gg Hh Ii Jj Kk Ll Mm
Nn Oo Pp Qq Rr Ss Tt Uu Vv Ww Xx Yy Zz

O is for octopus.

Octopuses hide during the day. At night, they hunt for crabs, clams, and oysters.

Aa Bb Cc Dd Ee Ff Gg Hh Ii Jj Kk Ll Mm Nn Oo **Pp** Qq Rr Ss Tt Uu Vv Ww Xx Yy Zz

P is for parrotfish.

Parrotfish have large teeth to bite coral. Smaller teeth in the throat grind coral into sand.

Q is for queen triggerfish.

Queen triggerfish seem to have wrinkles. These markings help triggerfish hide from other animals.

Aa Bb Cc Dd Ee Ff Gg Hh Ii Jj Kk Ll Mm Nn Oo Pp Qq Rr Ss Tt Uu Vv Ww Xx Yy Zz

R is for raccoon butterfly fish.

Raccoon butterfly fish move their bodies back and forth to swim. They glide through the water.

Aa Bb Cc Dd Ee Ff Gg Hh Ii Jj Kk Ll Mm
Nn Oo Pp Qq Rr Ss Tt Uu Vv Ww Xx Yy Zz

S is for sea horse.

Sea horses seem to stay in one place. But they do swim. The sea horse is one of the slowest fish in the world.

20

Aa Bb Cc Dd Ee Ff Gg Hh Ii Jj Kk Ll Mm Nn Oo Pp Qq Rr Ss **Tt** Uu Vv Ww Xx Yy Zz

T is for turtle.

Sea turtles have shells. Unlike other turtles, a sea turtle cannot pull its feet or head inside its shell.

Aa Bb Cc Dd Ee Ff Gg Hh Ii Jj Kk Ll Mm
Nn Oo Pp Qq Rr Ss Tt Uu Vv Ww Xx Yy Zz

U is for urchin.

Urchins have five teeth. They use them to bite algae off rocks.

22

Aa Bb Cc Dd Ee Ff Gg Hh Ii Jj Kk Ll Mm
Nn Oo Pp Qq Rr Ss Tt Uu Vv Ww Xx Yy Zz

V is for vase sponge.

Vase sponges are shaped like bowls or tubes. Some animals hide inside these underwater vases.

W is for walrus.

Walruses can swim underwater for up to 10 minutes. They crawl onto ice chunks or onto the shore to rest.

Aa Bb Cc Dd Ee Ff Gg Hh Ii Jj Kk Ll Mm Nn Oo Pp Qq Rr Ss Tt Uu Vv Ww Xx Yy Zz

X is for boxfish.

Boxfish swim slowly. Their strange shape makes it hard for boxfish to swim fast.

Aa Bb Cc Dd Ee Ff Gg Hh Ii Jj Kk Ll Mm Nn Oo Pp Qq Rr Ss Tt Uu Vv Ww Xx Yy Zz

Y is for yellow stingray.

Yellow stingrays have a tail they use to sting animals that come too close.

Z is for zooplankton.

Zooplankton drift in the ocean. Fish, shellfish, and whales eat zooplankton.

Ocean Life Facts

Anemone
- uses tentacles to catch food
- sometimes lives together with clownfish

Brittle star
- lives with no brain, head, or eyes
- has many tubes on each arm

Chocolate chip sea star
- also called "starfish"
- eats oysters, clams, and coral

Dolphin
- mammal that feeds milk to its young
- fins and flippers help it swim

Eel
- lives in saltwater or freshwater
- lays eggs

Frogfish
- lives near sponges
- swims in pairs

Great white shark
- uses nostrils to smell, not breathe
- female gives birth to pups

Hermit crab
- has one large pincer claw
- moves into a new shell as it grows

Indigo hamlet
- usually lives alone
- has blue stripes on its body

Jellyfish
- has a soft body without bones
- many tentacles help it sting prey

Killer whale
- is really the largest dolphin
- also called "sea wolf"

Lionfish
- darts quickly to catch fish
- swims in shallow water

Manatee
- breathes air above the water
- also called "sea cow"

Needlefish
- swims in warm water
- sometimes called "sea gar"

Octopus
- has one eye on each side of its head
- squirts ink when frightened

Parrotfish
- looks like it has a parrot's beak
- grinds sand

Queen triggerfish
- has a large head
- eats sea stars and urchins

Raccoon butterfly fish
- has black and white stripes
- usually swims with other butterfly fish

Sea horse
- uses tail to grab things
- female gives male her eggs

Turtle
- lives up to 80 years
- lays eggs in sand

Urchin
- eats kelp and other plants
- has an exoskeleton

Vase sponge
- water flows in and out
- grows in many shapes and colors

Walrus
- has two tusks
- uses whiskers to find food

Boxfish
- often has spots
- hides behind rocks

Yellow stingray
- hides on the ocean floor
- looks like it flies through the water

Zooplankton
- eats tiny plants
- made of larvae and eggs from sea life

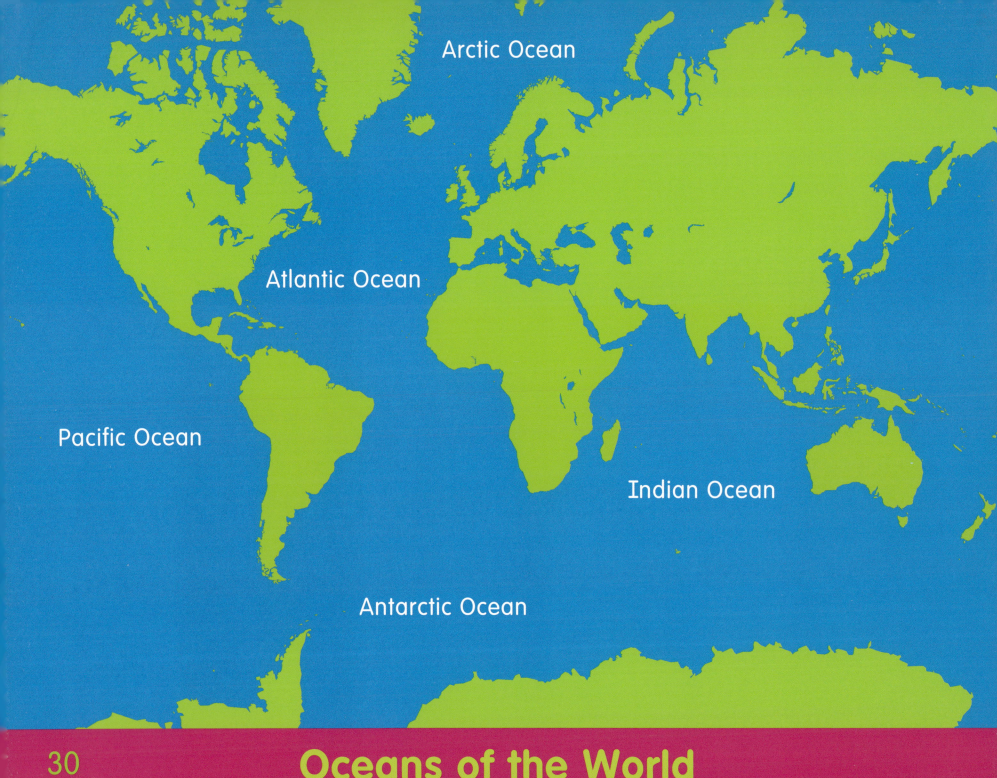

Words to Know

algae (AL-jee)—small plants without roots or stems; algae grow in water.

blowhole (BLOH-hohl)—a nostril in the top of the head of a whale.

mammal (MAM-uhl)—a warm-blooded animal that has a backbone; female mammals feed milk to their young.

spine (SPINE)—a hard, sharp, pointed growth

Read More

Burnard, Damon. *I Spy in the Ocean.* San Francisco: Chronicle Books, 2001.

Leonhardt, Alice. *Ocean Life: Tide Pool Creatures.* Pair-it Books. Austin, Texas: Steck-Vaughn, 2000.

Rose, Deborah Lee. *Into the A, B, Sea: An Ocean Alphabet.* New York: Scholastic Press, 2000.

Spencer, Carolyn. *Alphabet Sea.* Summerland Key, Fla.: Tortuga Books, 1999.

Internet Sites

Track down many sites about ocean life. Visit the FACT HOUND at *http://www.facthound.com*

IT IS EASY! IT IS FUN!

1) Go to *http://www.facthound.com*
2) Type in: 0736816844
3) Click on "FETCH IT" and FACT HOUND will find several links hand-picked by our editors.

Relax and let our pal FACT HOUND do the research for you!

Index

blowhole, 5
boxfish, 25
brittle star, 3

chocolate chip sea
 star, 4
coral, 2, 10, 17

dolphin, 5, 12

eel, 6

frogfish, 7

great white shark, 8

hermit crab, 9

ice, 24
indigo hamlet, 10

jellyfish, 11

killer whale, 12

lionfish, 13

mammals, 14
manatee, 14

needlefish, 15

ocean, 7, 27
octopus, 16

parrotfish, 17
plants, 2, 14

queen triggerfish, 18

raccoon butterfly
 fish, 19

sea anemone, 2
sea horse, 20
sea turtle, 21
shell, 9, 21
spine, 13
stingray, 26

teeth, 8, 17, 22

urchin, 22

vase sponge, 23

walrus, 24

zooplankton, 27

A+ Books are published by Capstone Press
P.O. Box 669, 151 Good Counsel Drive, Mankato, Minnesota 56002
www.capstonepress.com

© 2003 Capstone Press. All rights reserved.
No part of this publication may be reproduced in whole or in part, or stored in a retrieval system, or transmitted in any form or by any means, electronic, mechanical, photocopying, recording, or otherwise, without written permission of the publisher. For information regarding permission, write to Capstone Press, 151 Good Counsel Drive, P.O. Box 669, Dept. R, Mankato, Minnesota 56002.
Printed in the United States of America

1 2 3 4 5 6 08 07 06 05 04 03

Library of Congress Cataloging-in-Publication Data
Knox, Barbara.
 ABC under the sea: an ocean life alphabet book / by Barbara Knox.
 p. cm.—(Alphabet books)
 Summary: Introduces ocean creatures through photographs and brief text that describe one animal for each letter of the alphabet.
 Includes bibliographical references (p. 31) and index.
 ISBN-13: 978-0-7368-1684-7 (hardcover) ISBN-10: 0-7368-1684-4 (hardcover)
 ISBN-13: 978-1-4296-3102-0 (softcover pbk.) ISBN-10: 1-4296-3102-3 (softcover pbk.)
 1. Marine animals—Juvenile literature. 2. English language—Alphabet—Juvenile literature.
[1. Marine animals. 2. Alphabet.] 1. Title. II. Series: Alphabet books (Mankato, Minn.)
QL122.2 .K65 2003
591.77—dc21   2002015067

Credits
Sarah L. Schuette, editor; Heather Kindseth, designer; Patrick D. Dentinger, illustrator;
 Juliette Peters, cover production; Kelly Garvin, photo researcher

Photo Credits
Brian Parker/TOM STACK & ASSOCIATES, 11
Corbis/Stuart Westmorland, 2; Brandon D. Cole, 3; Hal Beral, 4, 9, 25; Kit Kittle, 6; Lawson
 Wood, 10; Amos Nachoum, 15; Stephen Frink, 16, 19, 21, 22, 23; Jeffrey L. Rotman, 17, 26;
 W. Perry Conway, 24; Douglas P. Wilson, 27
Creatas, 18
Digital Stock, 7, 8, 12, 14
Digital Vision, 20
Doug Perrine/Seapics.com/Innerspace Visions, cover
PhotoDisc, Inc., 5, 13

Note to Parents, Teachers, and Librarians
ABC Under the Sea uses color photographs and a nonfiction format to introduce children to various ocean life while building mastery of the alphabet. It is designed to be read aloud to a pre-reader or to be read independently by an early reader. The images help early readers and listeners understand the text and concepts discussed. The book encourages further learning by including the following sections: Ocean Life Facts, Words to Know, Read More, Internet Sites, and Index. Early readers may need assistance using these features.